Fifty Shades of BenGay

A Parody

LEAH CARSON

DEDICATION

To Tom, who bought the original *Fifty Shades*
(without knowing what it was about)
and got this whole thing rolling.

CHAPTER 1
GIRL MEETS HUNKALICIOUS BOY

Despite hours of backcombing and spritzing with White Rain Hair Spray, my beehive tops out at a mere 10 inches. I curse my hair and scowl at the mirror.

A pale, blue-eyed girl stares back at me. I have no idea who she is; my eyes are brown, and my nose is spiderwebbed with red capillaries from heavy drinking. Anyway, I only resorted to that mirror gimmick so I could describe myself while writing in the first person.

Dang it, why did Catherine Cadaver get blitzed at Stanley's Tap last night? She's supposed to interview a wealthy entrepreneur this morning for a feature in our school paper. Instead she's kneeling at the porcelain throne, puking her guts out.

So instead of studying for finals, I'm about to fill in for her, doing this stupid interview in stupid Delafield with this stupid rich guy who has some stupid company that earns billions of stupid dollars per year. Or something.

I can't believe I let Catherine Cadaver talk me into this. As my roommate and dearest friend, she knows I'm a hack writer. But she bribed me with a big bag of Doritos, so there you go.

To hide the drooping beehive, I decide to wear my puffy parka and pull the fur-lined hood over my head.

Boarding a Milwaukee County bus near our Cudahy rooming house, I seem to be the only passenger wearing a winter coat. Well, it is summer, after all. *Hey, people, gimme a break. Beauty school is a jungle; one bad-hair day can break you.*

Two transfers and three bus rides later, I get off at the park & ride at Highway C in Delafield and walk about a mile north.

You can't miss the headquarters of Mr. BenGay's global enterprise. It's a towering five-story building, all red brick and white cupolas. Well, actually, it's not *all* red brick and white cupolas, but I'm too lazy to describe it in further detail, so trust me: it's intimidating.

In the midst of a lobby that's all glass and steel, an attractive blonde woman sits behind the enormous reception desk, wearing the most sophisticated knit pantsuit I've ever seen. Wow. She must shop at Target.

"I'm here to see Mr. BenGay," I tell her. "Anesthesia Peel for Catherine Cadaver."

The blonde arches an eyebrow at me. "I see. May I take your…er…coat?"

"No, thanks." I clutch the olive fabric, pulling the hood closer to my face. "I'm, uh, awfully chilly today." As a graduating senior from Ma Baensch's Beauty School Class of 2013, I'd rather die than reveal my pitiful beehive.

"Sign in here," the blonde tells me. "Then take the stairs to the fifth floor." She hands me a visitor pass, which I clip to the lapel of my parka.

After climbing two flights, I'm sweating profusely. I unzip the parka just a few inches, wishing I hadn't worn my Beeriodic Table sweatshirt today.

About 20 minutes later, I stumble through the stairwell doors into the fifth floor, panting heavily. My ragged breathing echoes through the expansive lobby, which is all glass and steel except for the parts that aren't glass or steel. This time I'm met by another impeccable young blonde in a stunning outfit that looks like it's from Fashion Bug. I am way out of my element here.

She points to an arrangement of carved wood designer chairs. "Miss Peel, please wait here." Grateful, I plop into the nearest chair. One slender wooden leg gives way, and the chair collapses beneath me. *Dang, why do they make furniture so flimsy these days?* The fifth-floor blonde shoots me a dirty look and disappears into an office beyond.

I fish through my plastic Walmart bag for a Bic pen and Catherine Cadaver's list of questions. *Gol-dang it, I don't know anything about this guy. And the way Catherine Cadaver was spewing this morning, I couldn't get close enough to ask her.* The uncertainty makes me nervous. I start carving my initials in the designer chair.

"Ahem." The impeccable fifth-floor blonde appears next to me, frowning at my carving handiwork. I snap the penknife closed and scramble to my feet. A loose nail from a broken chair slat has snagged one heel of my rubber galoshes. I follow the blonde, dragging the chair slat. *Play it cool. Act like you meant to do that.*

"Mr. BenGay will see you now." The blonde points to a doorway. I cross the threshold – and trip over the doggone chair slat, doing a spectacular face plant into his office. The floor shakes as if a 4.5-magnitude earthquake just hit.

Crap! Double crap! Quadruple crap! No, wait, I skipped "triple crap." Grunting like a prize-winning sow at the State Fair, I get to my feet.

"Miss Cadaver." His long-fingered hands steady me. "Are you all right? Can I get you anything? Water? Coffee?" His gaze travels down to my thunder thighs. "A ten-course dinner?"

"I'm fine." I manage to extend my hand. We shake. His touch gives me an extraordinary tingle, like the time I retrieved my electric toothbrush from the bathtub without unplugging it first.

Wow. This guy is handsome. I'm talking major league hunk handsome. If he were a male dancer at a girls' night out, I'd be sticking a ten-dollar bill in his jock strap.

His hair is coppery, like plumbing in an old house down by Bay View. His eyes are as grey as unsoftened well water. And his fingers: so long and slender, reminiscent of someone from the movies. Who was that character? Oh, yes – E.T., the extra-terrestrial.

"I'm fine," I repeat. "But I'm not Catherine Cadaver. Right now she's puk—um, she's ill, so I'm filling in for her. I'm Anesthesia Peel."

"I see." What is he feeling? His expression gives no clue. Disgust? I'm used to that reaction. Curiosity? Or perhaps unbridled lust? Yes, unbridled lust, that must be it. How dare he! I pull the cap off my Bic pen and try to look journalistic. "Let's get started, shall we?" I glance at Catherine Cadaver's list of questions; most of them are stupid, so I decide to wing it. "How does it feel to be filthy rich?"

He smiles smoothly, as if people ask him this every day. "I love being rich," he says. "As for the filthy part, you'll just have to get to know me better."

Filthy, hmmm? Two can play this game. "Well, um…that's for me to know and you to find out." Immediately I realize this doesn't make sense. I fall back on Catherine Cadaver's list of questions. "What do you do when you're not working?"

He fixes me with his grey stare. It's so grey. Greylicious, really. "I sail. I fly. I stop bullets with my outstretched hand. I leap tall buildings in a single bound." His smile reveals perfect teeth. My heartbeat pounds, as if I've just glimpsed a fresh batch of donuts at Grebe's Bakery.

Good grief. I've got to get a grip. Why does he make me feel like a schoolgirl? Maybe because I am one. Without glancing at the question list, I punt: "What's your first name?"

"My, my." He frowns. "You've really done your homework, eh?"

"I told you – I'm just filling in for my roommate. I'd much rather be practicing for finals, maybe mixing up a batch of bluing chemical for the senior citizen special."

"Very well." He cocks his head to one side. "It's Crispin."

"Crispin? Your first name is Crispin?" I can't help but chortle. He glares. Oops. I check the question list again: "How would your friends describe you?"

"I don't have any friends."

"Okay, then, how would your enemies describe you?"

"Cold. Arrogant. Mean. Stingy. And extremely isolated. Basically, I hate people."

Naturally, I'm intrigued. "So why did you agree to this interview?"

"Two reasons. One: I'm a big benefactor of your school. I've endowed the Crispin BenGay humanitarian chair, as you may know."

"Of course." What kind of dummy does he think I am? "We use that chair all the time. I just gave somebody a perm yesterday while they were sitting in that chair." I push a wisp of sweaty parka fur off my lip. "And what's the other reason you agreed to this interview?"

"I couldn't get Catherine Cadaver off my back. She kept badgering my PR people."

"Don't they screen your calls?" It irks me to think that Catherine Cadaver got through to him. I've badgered plenty of former boyfriends, and none of them ever call *me* back.

"Yes," he says, "the PR department screens my calls, but I looked up Catherine on Facebook, and she seemed pretty hot." Oh-kaaayy. He's probably disappointed that I showed up instead.

Back to the question list: "Do you have any redeeming qualities whatsoever?"

"Of course. I invest heavily in algae farming. It's a humanitarian program. The millions of poor people in the world deserve something slimey and green to supplement their rice and rat meat." He smiles again. Whoo hoo, those pearly whites are irresistible.

He continues, "We have an excellent internship program here, Miss Peel. If you wish, I could get you a job in quality control. Something tells me you'd make a wonderful inspector on the algae assembly line."

"Thank you," I answer stiffly, "but I'm an English major with a minor in philosophy. Once I get my degree next week, I'll have more job offers than I can handle." I'd like to slam shut my interview book, but it's just a sheaf of papers, so I resort to crumpling it into a ball and throwing it on the floor. I stand up. "In addition to working in the hair salon of my choice, of course."

There's that smug smile again. Wow, this guy is one arrogant S.O.B. "Of course." He rises, extending his hand. "Until we meet again, Miss Peel."

As we shake hands once more, there's that odd tingle between us. Does he have a prank buzzer in his palm?

Moments later, I emerge into the streets of Delafield, panting with relief. What an arrogant, smug, supercilious, utterly hot and hunky….I've got to stop this train of thought. It's all Catherine Cadaver's fault, forcing me into this errand. Why do I keep doing favors for her? And for that matter, why do I refer to my supposed best friend by her first and last names?

Shaking my head, I hop onto the eastbound Badger Bus, hoping for an empty row or at least a seat that's not next to somebody with b.o.

**

I've worked at Dretzka's Department Store for years. It's got something for everybody – well, everybody whose fashion sense is frozen in 1974. But if your idea of ladies' petites starts at size 16, you'll feel like a princess at Dretzka's.

We're busy today, the beginning of the summer season, when ladies put away their corduroy overalls and start buying cotton housedresses. I throw myself into my work, and the rest of the day rushes by.

That night, as Catherine Cadaver and I watch "Bowling for Dollars," the doorbell rings. Standing on the doorstep is my good friend and token Hispanic, José Jimenez, clutching a bottle of Cuervo under one arm and a piñata under the other.

"José!" I motion for him to come in. "Welcome to my humble chapeau." It's an old inside joke from the movie "My Favorite Year." Unfortunately, José has never seen the movie, so the joke is one-sided.

"The word is *chateau*, Aña." He always says this. Humor is not his strong point. In fact, after knowing José for four years, I'm still trying to figure out whether he has a strong point. But now he's smiling. "Guess what? Mexican Fiesta said they'll feature my collection of chopped and channeled hot rods at the Summerfest grounds."

"José, that's fantastic!" I give him a careful A-frame hug. José wants to be my boyfriend, but he just doesn't turn me on. In fact, no guy has ever turned me on. I long for the stereotypical stomach-butterfly trembly swoony epiphany, but I only feel that way when I've spent too much time mixing hair dye. Oh, but wait – I did feel it this afternoon at BenGay Enterprises. Crap. I need to forget about that guy. *Fuhgeddaboutit, fuhgeddaboutit.*

The next morning, I'm deep into my work behind the counter at Dretzka's. Checking the inventory list, I notice we're low on babushkas and hairnets. Something catches my eye, and I look up – and there stands Crispin BenGay, staring at me hunkily.

Holy friggin' crap.

"Miss Peel. Fancy meeting you here." His grey eyes bore into mine. He's all outdoorsey and male-modelish. Is that a Lands' End sweater from Sears?

Wow, spare no expense. And those hiking boots totally look like they're from Gander Mountain. I gulp.

He smiles. "I was just in the neighborhood…" Huh? Nobody comes by this neighborhood unless they live within walking distance. "…and I need to do some shopping. It's so good to see you again, Miss Peel." His voice is warm and sweet, like Yoo-hoo chocolate drink.

I wipe the drool from my chin. "Please, call me Ana."

"Very well. Ana." He rubs his cheek with those long fingers of his. I wonder what else he has that's long.

My heart is in my throat, trying to escape from my mouth, which would be really bloody and gross. *Why is he here?* my subconscious screams. *Maybe he just likes to shop,* I inwardly scream back. *In the ladies' department at Dretzka's?* my subconscious shrieks. *He must be a cross-dresser.*

I manage to croak, "Can I help you find anything?"

"Yes," he says. "I need some strong rope, a blindfold, and a cattle prod."

What the — ?

"Do you know where I can get them?" he persists.

I manage to find my voice. "Try the Patrick Cudahy meatpacking plant." Turning on my heel, I stomp away, but he calls out:

"Ana!" I stop and turn around.

Slyly he asks, "Don't you need a photograph of me to go with that article for your school paper?"

"Well, yes…" *You're getting in over your head,* my subconscious warns.

Shut up, I retort. *Anyway, "subconscious" means "below the level of consciousness." We shouldn't even be talking.*

Very well, my subconscious replies primly. *I'll just send out the inner goddess.*

No! I cry. *Not the inner goddess!* But it's too late. My subconscious cackles fiendishly. No doubt she's descending to my inner depths, about to unleash the insufferable inner goddess….

An electric current jolts me. Startled, I focus: Crispin BenGay's incredible fingers are wrapped around my flabby upper arm. He lets go, but the buzz lingers. *Geez, this guy's a regular electric fence.*

"Ana?" He seems concerned in a sort of cool unconcerned way. "You were looking so dazed and stupid. I thought you were going to pass out."

"I'm fine." Taking a deep breath, I struggle to regain my composure. Is this love? Lust? Or just operant conditioning, like one of B.F. Skinner's experiments with rats, electric shocks and intermittent reinforcement?

Why does Crispin BenGay make me feel like a kid instead of a grown woman who can vote, drive a car, and out-drink most of the regulars at Stanley's Tap?

"Here." He seems a trifle impatient. I grasp the business card he offers, careful not to touch those electrically charged fingers. "Call my cell," he says. "We'll arrange a photo shoot. You bring the photographer. I'll bring…myself." He waggles his eyebrows so seductively that I almost wet my pants. "Laters, babe." He turns and walks out.

A heat wave suffuses my body. I'm barely able to totter to the ladies' room. After splashing cold water over my face and underarms, I study myself in the mirror. Sweet relief: I'm looking like myself again, spiderweb veins and all. Then I grin.

I've got a date with Crispin Sweetmeat BenGay.

Holy friggin' guacamole.

LEAH CARSON

CHAPTER 2
GETTING BUZZED

The Pfister Hotel in downtown Milwaukee has hosted countless celebrities over the years: Liberace, Albert the Alley Cat, Roland the Headless Thompson Gunner. And now the elegant hotel can add another luminary to this list: Crispin BenGay. For some reason he has rented the Pfister's Beer Baron Suite, even though his Delafield home is just a 40-minute drive away.

I guess when you're filthy rich, you can afford to piss away a fortune on a hotel room you don't need. Idly I pop another peanut into my mouth. We're sitting in the hotel's second-best lodging, the Shot-and-a-Beer Suite, waiting for Crispin to arrive for the photo shoot. Catherine Cadaver is biting her nails. José Jimenez fiddles nervously with the flashcubes of his antique Polaroid camera.

Crispin BenGay bursts through the door. I almost choke on a peanut. *Holy cannoli, this guy is hot.* His white shirt is open seductively at the neck. His grey flannel pants hang seductively from his hips. His coppery hair is seductively damp from a shower. The toes of his dress shoes peek out seductively beneath his pant hems. He's followed by an assistant who's all buzz cut and stubble. Unfortunately the buzz cut was done on his beard, and the stubble covers his head. Eeuuuwww.

Catherine Cadaver steps forward. "Mr. BenGay." With her businesslike manner, she seems immune to his utter seductuosity. "I'm Catherine Cadaver." As they shake hands, she shows no sign of feeling an electrical jolt. Maybe he isn't wearing the palm buzzer today.

She motions toward me. "And of course you already know Anesthesia Peel."

A hint of a smile crosses his lips. "Of course." He extends his hand, and we shake – *Owww! Another shock. Dang it!*

José hovers nearby. Since José has been sulking around all morning like

13

the would-be boyfriend he is, I half expect him to pull some macho stunt to one-up Crispin BenGay. But now that BenGay's actually here, José seems intimidated by his brilliance. "My name José Jimenez," he mutters, offering a brief handshake.

For the next 20 minutes, Catherine Cadaver directs the photo shoot, asking BenGay to sit here, stand there, lie on the bed, hang from the chandelier and so on. Finally, José runs out of flashcubes. The session over, both José and Catherine Cadaver shake hands with BenGay once more. He turns to me. "Would you walk with me, Ana?"

Holy heart attack. Walk? Me? Unsure what he's up to, I nevertheless follow him into the hallway. Mr. Stubbly Buzz Cut follows us. "Lurch," BenGay tells him, "take a hike." Buzzcut/Lurch nods, stomping away down the corridor.

"Ms. Peel, will you join me for coffee?"

I'm stunned. My jaw drops. BenGay extends a long, long index finger and lifts my jaw back into place.

I stammer, "Umm...I have to drive my friends home."

"Well, that's a lame excuse if I ever heard one." BenGay snaps his fingers. "Lurch!"

Buzzcut turns around and comes back to us. "Yes, master?"

"I want you to drive Miss Peel's friends home. Take the Bentley. On second thought, take the Aston Martin. No, wait, take the Rolls."

"Yes, master."

Again, Buzzcut lurches away. Crispin and I ride the elevator down to the lobby and walk outside. "Do you have a favorite coffee house in this area?" he asks.

"No," I say. "I'm not really into coffee."

"Then what's your pleasure?" There's that hint of a smile again. Are we talking about beverages, or...?

"Beer, mostly," I admit. "And hard liquor."

"Beer. Hmmm." He considers this for a moment, then hails a cab. He actually holds the door for me, unlike most of the schleppy guys I date, who won't even let me go first when we're boarding a city bus. Minutes later, the taxi brings us to Mader's German Restaurant.

Soon we are sharing a giant pretzel that's easily two feet in diameter. Our huge beer steins are filled with a dark, thick Franziskaner Weiss that gives me an immediate buzz. Crispin must feel it too, because he takes my hand and holds it. *Holy schnitzelgrüber!* Those long, long fingers wrap twice around mine.

"So, is José your boyfriend or what?" he asks.

I laugh so suddenly that beer spurts out my nose. "José...my boyfriend?" I gasp, wiping a corner of the white tablecloth across my face. "What gives you that idea?"

"He seemed a little jealous." Crispin sips his beer reflectively. "Whenever you weren't looking, he made obscene gestures at me."

I shake my head. "We're just friends."

"That's good to hear," Crispin says. "I don't like rivals."

Rivals? Whoa, he's moving awfully fast.

"Tell me about yourself, Ana." Crispin leans back, his elbow jostling the suit of armor behind him. It tips, crashing into a display of antique Black Forest woodcarvings and breaking a stained glass window. The manager rushes over, distraught. Crispin simply throws several $100 bills in the manager's direction and says, "I've got it covered."

He turns back to me and repeats, "Tell me about yourself, Ana." A weird grin spreads across his face. "Have you been tested lately for AIDS? What about syphillis and gonorrhea? And how do you feel about whips?"

All right, I've heard enough. "This date is over," I mutter between clenched teeth as I stomp toward the exit.

Hmmmph! I'm supposed to "put out" just because he bought me a giant pretzel and beer? What kind of cheap slut does he take me for? I expect at LEAST the sauerbraten platter before hopping in the sack on a first date.

I stride down the sidewalk, so angry I barely notice the roaring behind me, until suddenly – *whooosshhh!* A runaway garbage truck rushes past, mere inches away, as Crispin grabs me in a horse-collar tackle. I fall into his arms. The truck crashes into the front entrance of Mader's. I wonder whether they've got business-interruption insurance.

Crispin grasps me tightly against his chest. I inhale his scent, a blend of Hai Karate cologne and $100 bills. It's intoxicating.

"Are you okay?" he murmurs, tenderly wiping pretzel crumbs off my upper lip. Our eyes lock. His breath hitches. I wish this moment would last forever, or at least until I have to go pee from all the Franziskaner Weiss I just drank.

Time stands still. I focus on his lips. *Kiss me, you fool.* Crispin stares down at me, his eyes cloudy, his forehead damp, his hair stormy with a 50 percent chance of rain. He shakes his head.

"Anesthesia, you should stay away from me. I'm no good for you." He pushes me, forcing me to stand up straight. "Breathe, Anesthesia, breathe."

Breathe? He's got a lot of nerve, telling me to breathe. I shake my head, holding my breath deliberately.

"Breathe, I tell you!" he shouts.

Again I shake my head. My face is flushed. Pinpoints of light appear in my field of vision. It dawns on me that fainting here would mean falling into the gutter among the cigaret butts. Okay, I'll breathe.

I can barely bring myself to look at Crispin. *He wouldn't kiss me. He doesn't want me.* All that's left is to drag my wounded pride back home and drown my sorrow in a big bag of pork rinds.

"Goodbye," I whisper through my tears. "Thanks for the pretzel and beer." And Crispin BenGay, that schmuck, simply lets me walk away.

By the time I reach the bus stop, I'm bawling. And just when I think it can't get any worse, *she* appears.

My inner goddess.

"Boy, you really blew that one." She folds her arms across her chest, tapping the narrow toe of her leopard-skin stiletto heels. "If you weren't such a ditz, the two of you would be playing 'hide the wienerschnitzel' in his hotel room by now."

"Shut up," I mutter. A sob shakes my chest.

As usual, she ignores me. "Looks like you wore your purple striped Hot Topic thong for nothing," she sneers.

"Shut *up!*" I shriek. Other people waiting at the bus stop are giving me strange looks. I pull up the hood of my parka and tighten the drawstring until the opening around my face narrows to about three inches. It probably makes me look like an anteater, but I don't care. I don't care how I look. I don't care about anything. I just want to die. Okay, first eat a big bag of pork rinds, and then die.

***

By the next afternoon, I'm feeling a little better. Catherine Cadaver and I finished our final exams this morning. We plan to celebrate by going down to the Summerfest grounds for Mexican Fiesta.

The doorbell rings. I rush to the door, but as usual the United Parcel guy has hustled back to his truck before I get there. Geez, he's so paranoid, ever since the time I came to the door in my baby doll p.j.'s.

The package, addressed to me, bears no return address. Inside is a cellophane-wrapped cheese-and-sausage platter. A plain white card bears a handwritten note:

When life is stinkier than Limburger cheese, hang on – it's about to go from bad to wurst.

Immediately I know who sent this, and it infuriates me – but not enough to keep me from tearing open the cellophane and munching on a hunk of summer sausage.

Catherine Cadaver reads over my shoulder. "Oooh. He likes you, Ana."

"I shouldn't accept this. I'll have to send it back." Except I've already taken two big bites of sausage.

My inner goddess is picking her nose. "Too late," she says. "Might as well keep eating."

She's right. I grab a handful of cheese and head for my bedroom. What to wear for our night out? My Green Bay Packers sweatshirt, my Milwaukee Brewers jersey, or an elegant flannel plaid shirt from Farm & Fleet?

***

"Gee, José, I thought you were exhibiting your *cars*. Plural."

I'm feigning interest in José's cherry red hot rod, but piñatas keep bumping into my skull. So distracting.

"So did I, Aña." José shrugs. "But as soon as I drove up in this one, they said 'That's enough.'"

I can't help adding, "And I thought they'd be parked outside." The jalopy takes up way too much floor space in this tent of Hispanic arts and crafts.

Yet maybe it's best that he parked in here. It's friggin' freezing outdoors, with the wind howling off Lake Michigan. I'm so glad I wore all three of my fave tops: the sweatshirt, the jersey, *and* the flannel plaid.

José retrieves a jack from the trunk of his car. Placing it under the rear fender, he cranks until there's a couple feet of clearance. "Want to see the undercarriage?" he asks. "I detailed it myself this morning with Q-Tips and Bon Ami."

"Sure," I say. José removes his leather jacket and gallantly spreads it across the grass. I lie down on it, face up, and push myself under the car.

Instantly he's lying at my side – way too close. Uh-oh.

"Oh, Aña, Aña," José whispers in my ear. He grabs at my chest and comes up with a fistful of Packers sweatshirt.

"José, please." I push his hand away.

"I can't help myself, Aña." Again he gropes me, this time grabbing a handful of all three shirt layers.

"Cut it out, José. And stop calling me Aña. My name doesn't have a tilde."

José's taco breath nearly overwhelms me. He starts loosening his belt buckle. "I have another hot rod to show you."

"No way, José!"

"Sí, Aña. Oh, sí, sí, sí."

Suddenly I'm whisked out from under the car. I gasp. What…how….?

It's Crispin BenGay. He hauled me out by my feet. What's he doing here?

José whirls around and peers from underneath the bumper. His face darkens when he spots Crispin.

"I believe the lady said no, gearhead," Crispin snarls. He kicks the jack out from under the bumper. The hot rod falls, pinning José to the ground. "Oucho! Ooocho!" he cries.

Crispin grabs my hand. "Let's get out of here." He pulls me away from the piñata tent, past the Big ICE outdoor stage sponsored by U.S. Immigration and Customs Enforcement, and beyond the Careers in

Landscaping exhibit. Finally we reach the parking lot beneath the soaring Hoan Bridge.

Within moments, Buzzcut/Lurch pulls up in a quietly purring luxury car. I don't know whether it's the Bentley, the Aston Martin, or the Rolls. All I know is that Crispin BenGay is holding open the back door and motioning me inside. I can barely believe it. I'm about to ride in the back seat with Crispin Hunkalicious BenGay. With Crispin Hunkadelic BenGay. With Crispin Hunkydory –

"Are you getting in or not?" he growls.

I snap out of my reverie. "Um, yeah, sure." Flustered, I dive toward the door opening, but I'm coming in too high. My forehead strikes the roof. Flashes of light alternate with darkness. The darkness wins. As I pass out in Crispin's arms, the last thing I hear is his tender endearment:

"Clumsy idiot!"

CHAPTER 3
MR. WRONG

In my dreams, I'm drifting, drifting....I'm on the Edelweiss tour boat, cruising the Milwaukee River. The water level is high. Maybe they opened the deep tunnels for sewage overflow. The boat rocks back and forth, back and forth....

Gradually I awaken. I'm not on the Edelweiss after all. I'm in a waterbed. The surroundings seem oddly familiar. Wait a minute – this is Crispin BenGay's suite at the Pfister Hotel.

I don't remember coming here. The last thing I remember is hitting my head on the doorframe of his luxury car. Now I'm lying in his bed, wearing only panties and my 48FF cantilevered bra. No pants. No Packers sweatshirt or Brewers jersey or Farm & Fleet flannel plaid shirt. Holy flabby-pale-skin exposure.

The nightstand holds a bottle of Tylenol and a chilled can of V8 juice. What a control freak Crispin is. He won't even give me a chance to say "I coulda had a V8."

There's a knock on the door. Before I can say "Go away," Crispin enters the room. Obviously, His Hotness has been working out; he's all sweaty and muscular. My inner goddess is holding a vibrator and waving it like a traffic cop, gesturing toward Crispin's crotch.

"Breakfast is in 15 minutes," he says. "Don't be late." He points to a Goodwill bag on the chair. "There's a new outfit for you." He leaves, slamming the bedroom door behind him.

Warily I inspect the bag's contents. There's an enormous pair of purple jeans, a huge black and orange striped long-sleeved T-shirt, and a baggy 18XL pink sweatshirt with the original Walmart price tag still attached. They all fit perfectly. *How did he know?*

After donning my new outfit, I tiptoe into the suite's enormous living room. It's all overstuffed couches and other furnishings I'm too lazy to describe. At the far end, Crispin sits at a dining table. Room service has spread the table with enough food for a dozen people.

"I figured you'd be hungry," he says. I nod, and before too long I've devoured every last crumb of it.

Crispin watches with a bemused expression. He unfolds the foil wrapper from a small, dark object, and with his long, long, long fingers, he holds it out for me.

"Wafer-thin mint?" he asks.

"Umm, no thanks." I let out a huge belch. "I've had enough."

"All right, then. Let's get down to business."

Uh-oh. I should have known there was a price for all this. That breakfast spread alone would cost nearly $20 at IHOP. And then there's the new outfit....

"What are you doing in the next 24 hours?" he demands.

Boy, is he nosy. "Who wants to know?" I retort.

Shaking his head, he snaps, "Anesthesia, I don't have time for this. Thousands of people in my corporation are waiting for me to boss them around. We absolutely must make a billion dollars every hour and give most of it to the poor. So, how soon can I see you again? Are you working today?"

"Yes," I say, chastened. "Until eight o'clock tonight."

"I'll pick you up at Dretzka's at eight. We'll fly out to Delafield." He puts on a pinstriped blazer and picks up his car keys. "Let's go."

I follow him to the elevator. We're alone as the car heads down to the lobby. Crispin eyes me lustily, just like José looked at me last night under his hot rod.

Before I can declare "No way, José," Crispin pins me against the elevator wall, lips sucking my face like a lamprey eel, tongue exploring my mouth like a pet snake looking for feeder mice. Our tongues twine together in a slow, erotic dance that's all taste buds and saliva, all molars and canines, all scraps of food from my room service breakfast.

The elevator stops, and the doors slide open. Immediately Crispin jumps away from me as several businessmen board the car. I slither to the floor like a helping of warmed-over Jell-O. They pretend not to notice. Crispin examines his fingernails, seemingly unconcerned. How can he snap out of it so quickly?

Then he gives me a sideways glance and winks. My inner goddess is doing the Swan Lake Pas de Deux, dancing all the parts by herself.

**

The workday at Dretzka's drags on and on. I straighten racks of men's polyester leisure suits, sort piles of ladies' girdles, and stack bottles of white cream shoe polish.

Before I left for work, Catherine Cadaver prepared me for tonight's date. She forced me to shave my legs; it's been so long since my last shave that I used up six of her disposable razors. She plucked my brows; my unibrow is now two separate pieces. She even handed me an old washrag and ordered me to wash between my toes.

I feel ready for anything – but once again, Crispin BenGay takes me by surprise. Buzzcut Lurch drives us to a private hangar at Mitchell International, and Crispin helps me out of the car. I stare straight ahead, gaping.

Crispin is obviously pleased at my astonishment. "Surprised?"

"When y-you said we'll 'fly' to Delafield," I stammer, "I...I thought you had a private plane or something. Not..."

I gesture, at a loss for words.

"Not a zeppelin?" Crispin is actually smiling, so proud of his airship.

The zeppelin towers over us like a giant cigar. Wow, Crispin BenGay's very own personal zeppelin. I wonder what else he has that's huge.

We step into the basket. The pilot, seated up front, wears a severe uniform with a swastika on the cap. I feel a twinge of doubt. "Umm, this thing isn't going to burst into flames, is it?"

Crispin beams. "No. After that Hindenburg incident, flammable hydrogen in airships has been replaced by helium." The zeppelin rises into the night, almost completely silent.

"Oh, helium. Like in a party balloon." I try to sound sophisticated as the city lights pass beneath us. "Could we take a drag of it? It makes your voice sound funny. Kind of like Donald Duck."

Crispin gives me a soft *tsk-tsk.* "Oh, Anesthesia. What am I going to do with you?"

That's what I'd like to know.

A short while later, the airship descends to the zeppelin pad atop Crispin's condo building in Delafield. Crispin helps me out of the zeppelin. It's very windy atop this towering two-story building, but he steadies me as we head to an elevator that whisks us directly to the penthouse suite.

Inside it's all white furniture and dark wood and expensive original art and a bunch of other expensive stuff. There's a U-shaped sofa that could easily seat five dozen, and a dining set that seats 100.

"Wow," I blurt out, "quite a setup for a guy who hates people."

"I did it for the resale value," Crispin says. "For the same reason, I installed sixteen bathrooms. At this price point, you don't just build for yourself, but for the next filthy rich, selfish, wasteful buyer."

"I see," I murmur.

Crispin moves smoothly to the wet bar. "Something to drink?" he asks.

"Umm, yes, please." Now that zero hour is almost upon us, my palms are sweaty. "You got any Miller Genuine Draft?"

He smiles again. That's the third time this hour; it's making me nervous. "I thought we'd have some ridiculously expensive white wine. Is Domaine le Bondage all right with you?"

"Sure. Fine. Whatever."

He pours, then hands me a glass. Even this feels expensive – heavy crystal. I hope I don't drop it.

He holds up his own glass, and we clink the goblets together lightly. "To us," Crispin says. "To passion. To handcuffs."

Handcuffs?

"Excuse me." He sets his goblet on an expensive laquered-wood side table, not even bothering to put down a coaster. Now *that's* wealthy.

Crispin disappears into another room and returns holding a document. He looks a bit embarrassed. "If you're going to stay here tonight, you'll need to sign this first," he says. "My lawyer insists upon it."

I suppose I should read it, but the wine has already made me feel a bit stupid. "What does it say?"

"It's a nondisclosure agreement. You cannot disclose anything about us, to anyone. In particular, you cannot reveal particulars about my naughty bits."

"Oh." I hiccup. "Is that all? Sure, I'll sign." I grab the paper and pen he offers, scribbling my name on the dotted line. "There, satisfied? Now let's get it on. You know what they say: save a horse, ride a cowboy." Wow, I'm pretty clever tonight. Must be the wine.

"Not so fast," Crispin says. "I want you to see my playroom." He leads me downstairs. Through the wine fog, my mind registers the fact that he owns *both floors* of this condo. We reach a heavy green door.

"What's behind the green door?" I ask.

Crispin unlocks the door and opens it. "See for yourself."

CHAPTER 4
RED, RED ROOM

The first thing I notice in Crispin's secret room: on the far wall, a large X made of polished wood, with restraining cuffs on all four corners. I don't recall ever seeing anything like this in the Crate & Barrel catalog.

From an iron grid suspended from the ceiling hang all kinds of ropes, chains, Paula Deen copper pots and Rachael Ray aluminum pans. Curtain rods fastened to the wall are draped with riding crops, whips, and a toilet plunger.

An ornate mahogany bed dominates the room. It holds another set of handcuffs. *Hmm, Crispin must be a restless sleeper.*

Crispin watches me intently, obviously waiting for my reaction. "Oh," I manage to say, "this must be your workout room."

He snickers, and the term *Snidely Whiplash* pops into my mind. "This is the Room of Pain," he says darkly.

"Yeah," I say. "That's how I felt when I used to work out at the YMCA." Well, the one time I worked out there, anyway.

"So now you know my secret, Anesthesia," Crispin says. "I'll gain a great deal of pleasure – nay, even tidings of comfort and joy – from forcing you to submit to my will. The more you submit, the greater my pleasure."

"Hmmm. And what do I get out of it?" I ask.

"You get to watch me experience pleasure."

"Okay," I say. "Sounds like a plan."

"Good. Now I'll reveal your other big reward."

He leads me down the hall to a bedroom decorated in a circus theme. "This is where you'll sleep, Friday night through Sunday."

"Not with you?"

"No. I don't sleep with you. I don't sleep with anyone. And especially not in this hideous room. Now come, let's finish the paperwork."

Once again I follow him, this time to his study. He brings out a document that must be at least 500 pages long and drops it in my lap – ouch! I haven't even signed it, and we're already into the pain thing.

"These are my rules," Crispin says. "We can negotiate them, but only for changes that benefit me. They form a legal contract. I'll send you a copy for your files. Read this now, and we'll discuss it." Gee, what a hopeless romantic he is.

I check out the first page:

Rules
Obedience
    1. Ve haff vays of makink you talk.

    2. The Submissive will obey instructions from the Dominant, including but not limited to: sexual activity, dishwashing, toilet scrubbing, and sorting laundry. She will do so willingly and without kvetching.

Food
The Submissive will avoid pigging out. She will eat regularly from a prescribed list of edibles purchased at Whole Foods (Appendix 3). The Submissive will not snack between meals, with the exception of rice cakes. She is expressly forbidden from hiding distasteful foods (broccoli, cauliflower, etc.) on the tiny ledge beneath the dining table for purposes of pretending to have eaten them.

Personal Safety
The Submissive will not get blind drunk or stoned. She will not hitchhike or ride a mechanical bull.

Personal Qualities
The Submissive will conduct herself in a submissive manner at all times. She will walk five paces behind the Dominant, bow when he faces her, and respond "Yes, Anjin-san" to his commands.

Gosh. I haven't felt this restricted since I took confirmation classes at my Lutheran Church during junior high. "This is kind of…harsh," is all I can think to say.

"But wait. There's more." Crispin hands me a sheet of paper.

Hard Limits
No acts involving clowns or mimes.
No acts involving livestock, snakes, or migratory birds.

No acts involving fire extinguishers, Silly Putty, Mr. Bill figurines, or tar.

No farting within 10 inches of each other's face.

"So, what do you think?" he asks.

I grimace. *Think? If I was thinking, I wouldn't still be here.*

"Anything you want to add to the Hard Limits?" Crispin says. "Some disgusting things your previous lovers did that you never want to do again?"

"Not really." I might as well tell him. "I've never made love before."

Crispin gapes at me, flabbergasted. "You mean you're...a virgin?"

"Well, duh!" He doesn't have to put it so bluntly.

"Hmmm." He eyes me with a shrewd look. "Okay, since this is your first time, we'll start with the basics." He grabs me and pulls me against his hard body. *Oh, my. Is that a Sears Craftsman drill in your pocket, or are you glad to see me?*

My blood flames, and since I'm way too young for menopause, I figure this must be love. He sucks at my lower lip, then tugs it gently with his teeth, just like my old dog Taffy used to do.

Crispin leads me into his vast bedroom, where floor-to-ceiling windows without curtains or blinds look out on Delafield's sparkling nightscape. Fleetingly I wonder how many telescopes are trained on this room.

"Are you on the pill?" he asks.

"No," I say. "My ob-gyn talked me out of it." She'd said it was extremely unlikely that any guy would want to have sex with me.

"Never mind," Crispin says. "I've got condoms." A large cardboard box on the nightstand is stamped "TROJANS – ONE GROSS." He lifts the lid and pulls out one wrapped condom.

"Umm, since this is my first time," I ask, "could we start with a condom that's not gross?"

Crispin looks puzzled until he follows my gaze to the box. Then a smirk creases his lips. "*Gross* means the box holds one dozen dozen condoms. In other words, one hundred forty-four. Oh, Anesthesia." He caresses my cheek. "I've never had a partner who's so...ignorant. This will be interesting."

Crispin removes his expensive designer watch and places it on the nightstand. He removes his expensive designer jacket, placing it on a chair. He removes his expensive designer shoes and then takes off his socks individually (rather than both at once, like my mom taught me) and hangs them on a tiny antique sock frame.

My muscles clench, way down deep inside me. I haven't felt like this since I had too many chocolate martinis at Summerfest last year. Crispin leans down, kissing me, his lips firm and demanding and insistent and rather bossy, actually. Slowly he removes my pink 18XL sweatshirt, then my orange and black striped T-shirt, then my purple jeans. "There, that's better," he says. Maybe he didn't like the outfit after all. *Hmph. Well, he gave it to me.*

Crispin pushes me down onto the bed and gives me the once-over. "Wow, Anesthesia. I can't wait to boink you." *Holy Toledo. He's so debonair.* He dives on top of me.

I can't help myself. My body convulses in a shattering orgasm. The earth moves, the heavens part, and the "Hallelujah Chorus" erupts in my mind.

Crispin giggles. "Now it's my turn." He removes his briefs, pulls the condom over himself, yanks my legs apart and pushes his way into me.

"Ow!" I cry. "Jeez Louise, that hurts!"

"Get used to it," Crispin growls. "On the pain scale, this isn't even a one." His hard thrusts remind me of the time I tried – and failed – to climb over a barbed-wire fence on my cousin's farm in Oconomowoc.

Yet incredibly, through the pain, I feel another climax building inside me. Moments later I splinter into a million pieces beneath him. Geez, this sex stuff is really messy. I hope he employs a housekeeper to sweep up the splinters and the shattered parts and stuff.

Crispin comes inside me. More mess. I imagine his housekeeper stripping the bed and laundering the sheets, which makes me think of "The Help," which makes me think of chocolate pie, which reminds me that I'm hungry.

Crispin watches me speculatively. "You're biting your lip again." I can't tell whether he's feeling tender or irritated.

"I'm hungry," I admit.

"For more lovemaking?" He's grinning.

"No, for food." I could really go for a Palermo's pizza right now. Wonder what's in that enormous freezer in his enormous kitchen?

"You. Are. So. Sweet," he murmurs. "You. Are. Amazing."

"Don't people usually eat after making love?" In the movies they usually smoke after making love, but maybe we can start our own ritual.

"Come for me again, baby," Crispin growls. *All right, if that's what it takes*...I moan, grasping the covers, thrashing to and fro, pretending to come for the third time. He jumps on top of me and has his way with me again. Then we both fall asleep.

***

It's still dark when I awake, famished. Crispin is gone. *That figures.* From somewhere I hear the lilting notes of an accordion. I wrap the king-size duvet around myself and, though it doesn't completely cover my bare ass, I pad down the hall toward the music.

Crispin stands naked, playing his accordion, completely lost in the "Beer Barrel Polka." I pad quietly into the room. Might as well keep padding while I'm at it. He finally notices me and stops playing.

"Sorry," I say. "I didn't mean to disturb you."

He sets the accordion on a sequined bandstand labeled *Lawrence Welk All-Star Music Camp.* "That's all right," he says. "I'm already disturbed. Melancholy, sad, forlorn, unfathomable and despondent."

"Ah," I whisper. "Everything I've always wanted in a man."

We go back to bed. Crispin sleeps way over on the other side, as far from me as possible, like the melancholy, sad, forlorn, unfathomable and despondent lover – with an enormous *schwanstücker* – that he is.

***

Crispin is asleep the next morning as dawn creeps through the tall windows. Slipping out of bed, still barefoot, I pad into his enormous walk-in closet and check out his expensive designer suits, then pad into his enormous bathroom and pee in his enormous Kohler designer toilet. Finally I pad into his enormous gourmet kitchen.

Everything is so sleek and expensive: state-of-the-art restaurant style gas range, huge SubZero refrigerator/freezer, granite countertops, and a steel sink big enough to wash a 300-pound turkey. Too bad I don't cook. Where's the nearest McDonald's? I'll get breakfast for two at the drive-through.

Crispin appears in the doorway. He yawns, scratching the drop-seat of his designer pajamas. "In there," he says, pointing at the freezer.

I open the freezer door and discover a stack of Swanson frozen breakfast entrees. Gratefully I pull out several and pop them into the microwave.

We eat in silence. *I guess he's not a morning person.* Considering he just deflowered me last night, though, it would be nice to hear some sweet nothings. Crispin finishes the last of his French toast and mutters, "So, you wanna take a bath together?"

"Why?" I blurt out. "Do I smell bad?"

"Not at all." He smiles, and my heart does a triple back handspring followed by a side aerial and sticks the landing.

Crispin leads me to the enormous bathroom. The tub is made of white stone. It's very designer and is, of course, enormous – which may be a lame description, but frankly, I'm not paying much attention to the bathtub; Crispin has removed his pajama bottoms, and I'm agog at something else that's enormous.

He turns on the hot water tap and throws in a handful of Mr. Bubble bath soap. He helps me down the steps into the tub as it fills. "Turn around and face me," he orders. Remembering the 500-page contract, I comply. *Might as well get used to taking orders.*

"Anesthesia, I know your lip is very tasty," Crispin growls, "but will you please stop biting it? You look like a four-year-old. It reminds me of that time I was charged with – well, never mind. Just stop biting your lip."

He pushes me roughly, and I sit down. The water and the bubbles are already rising high in the tub. Crispin eyes the surface, takes a step back, and does a triple lindy into the water. I'm especially impressed that he does this without any diving boards.

He swims a couple of laps, stops behind me, and grabs my boobs. I inhale sharply as his long, long fingers knead them, taking no prisoners, whatever that means. "Turn around and face me," he orders again. His enormous erection stares me in the face.

"I'd like to introduce you to my very favorite body part," he says. "It goes by many names: dick, johnson, one-eyed trouser snake, and so on. I'm very attached to this."

"That's good," I manage to croak, " 'cause otherwise it might fall off." I can't believe this enormous thing was inside me not long ago. No wonder my innards feel like overcooked spaghetti. Is he related to Sonny Corleone?

I decide to impress him with my versatility. *I may have been a virgin until last night, but I've tramped around with plenty of guys before you.* I give him a hand job, then a blow job, then a lube and tire rotation. My inner goddess congratulates me: Mr. Goodwrench here is panting like a horny teenager.

We move back to the bedroom. Crispin binds my wrists with a long grey silk tie. He starts kissing me all over, which gives me a warm glow way down *there*, in the Feminine Region That Has No Name. When his mouth approaches that forbidden territory, I let go, screaming bloody murder. The force of my climax renders everything else null and void, like a General Mills cereal coupon past its expiration date.

We lie together for a few minutes, until Crispin murmurs, "Come for me, baby."

Huh? "I just did," I whisper.

"Well, I'm ordering you to come again," he says, rolling atop me and boinking my sore nether region. I fake another climax as quickly as I dare, hoping it's believable. Finally he climaxes and sags atop me, his full weight pressing me about a foot into the mattress. I realize that I would do anything for this man…or at least, I'd do anything to get him off me before I suffocate. His snore rattles my ear. *Uh-oh.*

Suddenly another sound breaks our romantic idyll. Voices bounce in the hallway just outside the bedroom door.

"But why is he still in bed? He never sleeps late. He's always up early with some nefarious capitalist scheme to steal from the downtrodden middle class and give to the even more downtrodden Third World poor."

"Mrs. BenGay. Please!"

"Lurch, get out of my way. You can't stand between me and my son."

"Mrs. BenGay, he's not alone."

"I know that. He always sleeps with his ticker-tape machine."

"No, I mean – there's a woman in there with him."

"Oh." Her voice reflects disbelief, even shock. "His stockbroker?"

Crispin grimaces. "Crapola. It's my mother."

CHAPTER 5
MOMMY DEAREST

Crispin puts on his clothes and rushes out to run interference. I don my purple pants and pink sweatshirt. When I reach the living room, a sandy-haired woman is standing next to him. Either this is Crispin's mother, or Lurch had a sex-change operation last night.

She's impeccably attired – unlike most of my Cudahy friends' mothers, who merely get dressed. She wears a camel-colored wool skirt and sweater with matching shoes and purse. I remember seeing this ensemble in the Coldwater Creek catalogs we use in our outhouse. *Holy Hohenzollern, this family is rich beyond imagining.*

"Mother, this is Anesthesia Peel," Crispin says. "Anesthesia, this is my mother, Dr. Grace Brandenburg-Bayreuth of Prussia." She smiles warmly and holds out her hand. I kiss her ring.

"You may call me mum, as in hum," she says, "not ma'am, as in ham. We'll skip the 'your Majesty' part."

"Yes, mum." I curtsy.

"Crispin," she says, turning to her son, "I wanted to take you shopping at Brooks Brothers, but I can see you've got better things to do." She winks broadly at both of us. "So I'll just be going now. Lurch!" He appears out of nowhere. "Summon my coach, please."

"Yes, mum." Lurch disappears again.

When Her Majesty Dr. Grace Bumble-Whatever has left with Lurch, Crispin's mood turns moody. He retrieves the 500-page contract, sealed in a Western States side seam envelope, and hands it to me.

"Read this, and do some research so you'll know what you're in for."

"Research?" I repeat dumbly.

"It's amazing what you can find on the Internet."

Oh, crappy-crap-crap. I stare at my feet. Crispin notices my hesitation: "What is it?"

"I don't have a computer," I mumble.

"Then surf with your laptop," Crispin snaps.

"I don't have a laptop either. Or an iPad." Dang it. I knew this would catch up with me sooner or later.

Crispin frowns, crossing his arms over his chest. "Let me get this straight. You're about to graduate from college, and you don't have your own PC, laptop or tablet?"

"Yup." I try to sound breezy, but I feel like a relic of the '50s – which, considering where I live and where I work, is exactly right. "I've been using a computer at the public library, whenever I can grab a workstation that's not monopolized by some dirty old man."

"Never mind. I'll buy you a computer." Crispin picks up his car keys. "I'm taking you home. Let's go."

I grab my purse and join him in the townhouse elevator. As the door slides shut, he adds, "For cripe's sake, stop biting your lip. That is *so* annoying."

The elevator door opens into an underground garage. Several expensive autos lined up across the smooth concrete all have variations of *Crispin* on their vanity plates. One car in particular, a sleek black sporty number, is so fascinating I don't even notice the make and model. Let's just say it's enormous and expensive.

He gets in beside me. "So, what kind of car is this?" I chirp.

"It's an import," he says mysteriously. "It gets 2.5 miles per gallon. Impressed?"

"Definitely." But a few minutes later, I'm seriously less impressed. Riding in a convertible is a lot less fun than it looks. My hair whips in the wind, blinding me, and I must clamp my lips together to avoid getting bugs in my teeth.

Crispin decides to stop for lunch at a small, intimate restaurant housed in a wooden chalet in the middle of a forest. I'm thinking *Hansel and Gretel*. Hearing Crispin order the Two Kids Special does little to ease my fears. Then he grins gorgeously at me, and my stomach pole-vaults over my spleen without even bothering to put on a safety helmet.

The soup course arrives. I'm relieved not to find any little fingers or toes floating in it. Crispin still seems moody; maybe I should make small talk. "So," I ask, "how long have you been into this S&M stuff?"

He frowns for a moment and then says, "When I was fifteen, one of my mother's friends seduced me."

"Oh." *Fifteen?* "Isn't that illegal?"

Crispin shakes his head. "We lived in San Francisco at the time." He stares off into space. "Mrs. Robinson was the dominant, I was the submissive. It went on all through my college years." Wow, he's really opening up to me. I keep nodding, hoping not to break the spell. "We grew very close. We had secret passwords like *koo-koo-kachoo*, and a special whip she reserved just for me." He notices I've stopped eating. "Eat, Anesthesia," he orders.

"I'm not hungry," I say. "Stories about child molesters sorta make me lose my appetite."

His face turns red. "Eat," he orders again. Cowed, I pick up my spoon and slurp the soup. It's weird to have somebody tell me to eat. People are always telling me to stop eating, usually around my third or fourth helping.

We are both quiet as we continue the drive home. I'm wondering what I'm getting into here. Crispin — well, I have no idea what he's thinking. Maybe return on investment with algae.

When he drops me off at our flat, Crispin mumbles something about taking me out to dinner Wednesday night. Yeah, whatever. I hope he comes up with a better dinner spot this time.

I walk through our door, and my spirits plummet; I'm about to face the Catherine Cadaver Inquisition.

"So, how was it?" she demands. "Did he nail you? How many times? Which positions? What else did you do? How big is he?"

"Catherine Cadaver. Really." I roll my eyes. "It's none of your beeswax."

"Hmmph." In the middle of the living room there's a big packing box; we're moving to Delafield right after graduation. Catherine Cadaver tosses a lamp, lampshade and all, into the box. "By the way, while you were away with Mr. Moneybags, I've been getting it on with his brother, Elliott Ness."

"Really? I didn't know he had a brother."

"Well, he does. Oh — and José has been calling for you. About once every three minutes." Not only are my computer habits Stone Age, but we're also the only twentysomethings in the modern world who still have a landline. On cue, the phone rings.

Sighing, I pick it up. "Hello."

"Aña! My name José Jimenez."

"Yes, José, I know. What do you want?"

"Aña, I want to apologize most sincerely for my behavior at Mexican Fiesta. I had too many margaritas, and I got carried away. I am most sorry for taking advantage of your friendship."

"I forgive you, José."

"Bueno! Then you will meet me for a reconciliation dinner? How about the Motel 6 on Howard Avenue?"

I hang up. Seconds later, the phone rings again. I yank the jack out of the wall. Then I help Catherine Cadaver pack our belongings.

Pretty soon, all that's left in the room are the couch, the TV, and the dining table. We've even removed the old towels stuffed in cracks around the window to keep out smells from the meat-packing plant on Layton Avenue.

Late that night, I lock myself in my bedroom and open my backpack. There it is: the 500-page contract Crispin gave me. This is scarier than any report card…scarier than the disciplinary updates our Pioneer Girls troop leader sent home to my mom…scarier, even, than the notice that I'd been suspended from Vacation Bible School. Taking a deep breath, I open the envelope.

CHAPTER 6
THE DOTTED LINE

Simply tearing open the envelope makes my heart pound. I take this to mean I'm out of shape.

Contract
Made this _____ day of _____, 2013
between
Crispin BenGay, Delafield WI ("the Dominant") and
Anesthesia Peel, Cudahy WI ("the Submissive")

The parties agree as follows:

The fundamental purpose of this contract is to allow the Submissive to experience the pleasures of being abused, injured, insulted, bossed around, confined, and otherwise mistreated by the Dominant.

This contract shall be effective for three calendar months ("the Term") from the contract date, which period shall include any ridiculous made-up federal holidays when the Post Office is closed.

The Submissive shall make herself available to the Dominant from Friday evenings through Sunday afternoons during the Term. The Dominant may use the Submissive's body in any manner. The Dominant may spank, whip, flog, pinch, slap, or hornswoggle the Submissive. The Dominant may use Saran Wrap, Krazy Glue, Marshmallow Peeps, 3-in-1 Oil, or duct tape while disciplining the

Submissive. In case of injury, the Dominant will supply the Submissive with latex-free bandages.

The Dominant shall not loan the Submissive to another Dominant unless said other Dominant is a certified member of the SubmissiveSwap™ program.

The Submissive accepts that the Dominant is her master, the Thirteenth Amendment to the United States Constitution notwithstanding. The Submissive agrees to obey the Dominant's commands without sulking, muttering, dragging her feet, or giving him the finger.

The Submissive is expressly forbidden from biting her lip unless instructed to do so by the Dominant.

The Submissive shall lose some weight, for Pete's sake. To aid this process, the Dominant shall provide the Submissive with a personal trainer for five hour-long sessions per week.

The Submissive shall not look directly into the Dominant's eyes or at his crotch without permission. The Submissive shall address the Dominant only as *Sir, Mr. BenGay, Anjin-san, Your Highness,* or other titles the Dominant might cook up.

Should the Dominant demand some truly perverse activities or inflict unrelenting pain, the Submissive may use the safeword "Tatanka" as a signal that the Submissive has just about had it. Further, the Submissive may use the safeword "Rosebud" to alert the Dominant that the Submissive is completely fed up and ready to shoot the Dominant. When the Submissive says the latter safeword, the Dominant will immediately cease action and take a chill pill.

We the undersigned have read and understood the loony provisions of this contract and acknowledge by our signatures that we're sufficiently warped to proceed.

_____

The Dominant: Crispin BenGay   (date)

_____

The Submissive: Anesthesia Peel (date)

I'm stunned. This is insane. Barbaric. *Five hours of exercise every week?*

My inner goddess is slashing her wrists. To think that Prince Charming is into slavery – ugh! I put on my Potawatomie Bingo Casino nightshirt, crawl into bed with a big bag of pork rinds, and eat myself to sleep.

***

When I get up the next morning, Catherine Cadaver informs me that one of Crispin's minions has delivered my new laptop computer and set it up for me. He even got me an email address: Luv2Bflogged@CrispinBenGayDominant.com.

Wow, my very own email account. I feel so modern. I'll add this to my resume, for sure.

I carry the laptop into my bedroom and fire it up. Cool – there's already a message from Crispin.

From: Crispin BenGay
Subject: Warning
Date: June 3, 2013
To: Anesthesia Peel

I forgot to mention: if you get any emails about Nigerian investment schemes, don't click on the links.

Crispin BenGay
CEO, BenGay Evil Monolithic Enterprises, Inc.

I can't help smiling. My first email love note! I type a reply.

From: Anesthesia Peel
Subject: Cute kittens
Date: June 3, 2013
To: Crispin BenGay

Thought you'd like these. Soooooo cute.

Anesthesia

I attach JPGs of a dozen adorable kitten photos, like I've seen Catherine

Cadaver do with her emails. I hit "send," feeling downright cosmopolitan.

Next I send him a collection of cute puppy photos, and then a third email that links to a YouTube video about an elephant and a cockroach that bonded when they met in an animal sanctuary.

Within minutes, a new email appears on my screen.

From: Crispin BenGay
Subject: Cuteness
Date: June 3, 2013
To: Anesthesia Peel

Stop sending me this shit. You're supposed to be researching S&M, bondage and the like. Use Google. If you don't know about Google, ask your roommate.

Crispin BenGay
CEO, BenGay Evil Monolithic Enterprises, Inc.

Hmmph. He doesn't have to get so bossy. But he did give me this computer, after all, so I'm obligated to do some research on bondage and discipline. I open Google and check out the topics.

An hour later, I'm nauseated. I mean, seriously nauseated. He really expects us to do this stuff? With whips and chains and a toilet plunger? It sounds more painful than getting my teeth cleaned, which I stopped doing about eight years ago.

He may be the hottest man on the planet, and I certainly don't want him to stop boinking me, but this S&M is for the birds.

Hey, maybe if I pretend we're through, he'll be so anxious to win me back that he'll forget about the contract. Then we can simply have nice, lovely sexual relations without all that pain and suffering.

From: Anesthesia Peel
Subject: Buh-bye
Date: June 3, 2013
To: Crispin BenGay

About our "deal":
Thanks, but no thanks.

Ana

P.S. Can I keep the laptop?

Ten minutes later, he still hasn't answered. It's making me nervous. Maybe he didn't get the "buh-bye" joke. Or was I joking? I'm not even sure. I certainly wasn't joking about keeping the laptop.

To pass time, I pick up the 500-page contract and read it again. Hmmm, maybe this would be OK, with some changes. I cross out *spank, whip, flog, pinch, slap, or hornswoggle* and write in *tickle*. Then I draw a big X over the whole weight-loss and personal trainer paragraph.

Oh, who am I kidding? Mr. Control Freak won't go for these changes. I start doodling in the margins of the contract. I draw a heart, a smiley face, and a lyger. It's not bad. I hold it up to admire my handiwork – and there, beyond the page, standing in the doorway of my bedroom, is Crispin BenGay.

Holy mother of pearl. He wears a white linen shirt that probably costs more than I make in a year at Dretzka's. His pants hang seductively from his hips – so unlike most of my boyfriends, whose belts are buried beneath their overhanging beer bellies.

"Hello, Anesthesia," he says cooly. "I hope you don't think I'm stalking you or anything…."

"N-n-no, not at all," I manage. *If I jump out the window, will the fall kill me? Probably not. We live on the first floor.*

"…But I thought your email deserved a personal reply." He locks the bedroom door and pulls a grey silk tie from his pocket. "May I tie you to the bed?"

Panic ripples through my veins. *I haven't changed my underwear in two days.*

He must sense my unease. "I'll make it worth your while." He smiles his debonair Crispin BenGay smile. "Shall we say – a box of vintage 2012 Hostess Twinkies?"

I melt. He pushes me onto the bed, fastens my wrists together, and ties them to the headboard.

"Don't move a muscle, Anesthesia, or I shall punish you," he says. "Don't make a sound, or I shall gag you."

"Hey! I haven't signed your contract yet." But Crispin obviously sees through my protests. *You had me at "Twinkies."*

Crispin lowers the zipper on his pants. I stare, transfixed. I'm all deer/headlights, moth/flame, magnet/refrigerator. Desire – intense, smoldering, like liquid hot magma – shoots through The Region That Has No Name inside me.

His mouth finds mine, which isn't hard, considering how big my mouth is. His tongue claims and possesses my mouth; I wonder if he'll give it back to me in time for those Twinkies.

Crispin starts pulling my nightshirt up over my head, but it gets stuck, so he leaves it there, covering my eyes.

"I'm going to get a drink," he growls.

Oh, yeah? That is SO rude. Going out to the tavern in the middle of – but within moments he's back. I hear his pants drop to the floor, and then he's on the bed, straddling me. I hear the familiar, unmistakeable *click-pop* of a beer can being opened, the soundtrack of my former love life.

"Open your mouth," he whispers. He leans down and kisses me, pouring beer from his mouth into mine as he does so. Maybe he thinks this is romantic in a kinky sort of way, but I've been there, done that with most of the drunks I go out with.

Still, it's beer. I smile, hoping he'll give me more. Even warmed-over beer, like a robin regurgitating worms for its babies, is better than no beer at all.

He tugs at my nightshirt again, harder and harder, yanking my ears upward, until finally the shirt pops off my head. *Ouch. This wasn't in the contract. Which I haven't even signed yet.*

Never mind. Now that I can see his neggid body, I'm like a golf ball, my rubber bands all wound up and waiting to explode at the touch of his huge driver.

Crispin grabs me by the hair and flips me over. *Oooowwww! You're pulling my HAIR, sicko.* He shoves his one-eyed trouser snake into me and, thankfully, lets go of my hair.

I come immediately – once, twice, three times. No, four times. No, wait, five times. Crispin boinks me harder and harder, and the feeling builds inside me again...oh, oh, oh...surely I can't...oh no....stop calling me Shirley...*Aaaaaaaiiiiieeee!* Once again I come, shattering into microscopic fragments. How in the world will I clean this up? We'll forfeit our damage deposit when we move out of the apartment.

Then Crispin releases himself into me. Eccchhh. Now I have to wash the sheets, too.

Crispin hops up and gets dressed in a flash. "See you Wednesday." He heads for the door.

"Hey!" I call. He turns around.

"Could you, like, untie me?" I ask, trying not to look as awkward as I feel.

He grins devilishly, returns to the bed, loosens the grey tie and sticks it in his pocket. Then he turns and leaves.

I'm left lying on the bed, feeling totally bereft. *I never got my Twinkies.*

CHAPTER 7
DIRTY SECRETS

On Wednesday, our date does not go well.

Crispin refuses to change the contract wording to *tickle* from *spank, whip, flog,* etc. He won't even discuss my suggestion about dropping the weight-loss/personal trainer thing. And when we're leaving, as the valet brings my car to the restaurant entrance and Crispin sees it's a beat-up Corvair and learns I've nicknamed it Gertrude, he laughs in my face.

Oh, my. I am SO in love with this man.

Luckily, the next day is Thursday – graduation day. Things can't help but get better. I'll claim my diploma and become officially overqualified for a job at McDonald's. What's more, I'll get to hear Crispin's speech to our graduating class at Ma Baensch's Beauty School. As a major benefactor, he's been invited to come and bore everybody out of their wits.

In the auditorium, I settle into my seat, black graduation gown clinging to my...um...curves. Good thing the rental company had one gown left in size XXL. Unfortunately, it makes me look like the ocean liner *Queen Mary*.

Catherine Cadaver is seated onstage, along with various professors from our school. And oooh, there's Crispin. Is he wearing...oh, my gosh...that grey tie. The one he used on me in the bedroom, to bind my wrists. I hope he washed the beer stains out of it.

Catherine Cadaver, our valedictorian, speaks first. Her theme is "What's Next After Graduation?" How original. I'm sure she'll be a huge success in her chosen career as a television news anchor. With her cute features, heavy makeup, subtly highlighted blonde hair and perfectly manicured nails, she's got what it takes to deliver News You Can Count On. She also reads brilliantly from a teleprompter and can even point to a weather graphic.

Polite applause ripples through the crowd as Catherine Cadaver finishes her speech. She waves and blows kisses at the audience.

When Crispin takes the podium, my nether regions tingle in anticipation. Surely this will go down as one of the greatest speeches in history. In my mind, Crispin's sexy baritone rings out with words for the ages:

"Friends, Romans, countrymen, lend me your vaginas."

"Ask not what your country can do for you. Ask what you can do for me."

"*Ich bin ein schmuck* who enjoys flogging women."

"Give me liberty, or give me total world domination."

"Never was so much owed by so many to so few – that's the story of my holding company."

"Our world is founded on four essential freedoms: freedom of speech, freedom of worship, freedom from want, and freedom to apply nipple clamps to our mistresses."

Applause fills the auditorium. My head snaps up, and I realize I've daydreamed through Crispin's actual speech. Oh, well, I'm sure it was brilliant.

Awarding the diplomas takes forever. Finally my name is called, and I stride across the stage, trying to look graceful rather than cruise liner-ish. Crispin himself is handing out the certificates.

I reach for my diploma. He lets me grasp it but doesn't let go. "So, will you be my submissive?" he mutters.

I glance sideways at the stage full of beauty professors and the auditorium full of beauty grads. "Can we talk about this later?" I whisper, tugging my diploma. He won't budge.

"I'm tired of waiting," he says through gritted teeth. "You lust after my body. You obviously enjoyed being tied to your bed. So what's the problem?"

The line of students is backing up behind me. "I'm just not sure," I mutter.

Students waiting in line turn rowdy: "Hey, get a move on!" "What's the holdup?" "Can't tell. The fat chick is in the way."

Crispin maintains a firm grip on my diploma. "Well?" His eyes bore into mine.

Oh, for goodness' sake. "All right," I say. "I'll try it. Now give me my friggin' diploma."

A triumphant expression lights up his face as he lets go of the diploma. I clutch it to my chest and scurry away. "About time!" somebody yells.

***

The next night, Crispin visits. We're about to discuss our contract. He's brought along some Wild Turkey, but all the glassware has been packed for moving day, so we'll have to chug the bourbon straight from the bottle. Works for me.

Before long, I'm buzzed. Crispin, who's been studying me closely, takes advantage of the moment to hand me a new list.

Soft Limits
Methods of inducing pain:
--whipping
--spanking
--forced watching of "Petticoat Junction" reruns
--clamping naughty bits
--listening to off-key sopranos in a church choir
--getting stuck behind a car going 5 mph under the speed limit
--wearing pantyhose

There's more, but the room has started spinning. I set the paper down.
"Everything all right?" Crispin asks.
"Fine," I gasp. "Could you open a window or something?"
Crispin obliges, sliding open the bottom pane. Immediately the familiar scent of the packing house wafts into our living room.

This is the moment of truth. The scene at graduation convinced me that Crispin is fed up. If I don't agree to the contract tonight, he'll walk away and never come back.

My inner goddess has passed out; no help there. I try to summon my subconscious, but she's still ticked off from my lecture about "sub" and "conscious." She sticks out her tongue and refuses to speak.

I feel myself weakening. "Well…"
"Come on, Anesthesia," Crispin breathes. "Say you'll be mine, all mine, to have and to hold and to hurt."
"I dunno…"
"Come here." He reaches out. Reluctantly, I grasp his hand. He tries to pull me off the couch, but my sheer mass drags him downward. He clasps my wrist with his other hand and hauls with all his strength, finally pulling me up.

Crispin leads me outside. "Look." He points. "My graduation gift for you." Parked at the curb is a brand new red BMW.

"Wow! A car!! You bought me a car!!!" I let loose a high-pitched scream that sets off the car alarm, and the Beamer starts honking, its headlights blinking on and off.

"A new car!!!!" I shriek. "Yes, Crispin!!!!! I will be your submissive!!!!!!"
I jump into Crispin's arms. The force nearly knocks him over.

"Let's go inside," Crispin suggests. "I want to boink you, but not with the neighbors watching." All of this commotion has brought out curious

women in housedresses and men in grubby t-shirts and jeans. I wave
merrily at them as Crispin leads me back inside, to my bedroom.

Desire courses through my blood and settles in that dark unmentionable
spot I still can't bring myself to name. Crispin begins unbuttoning my dress,
but it takes too long, so from out of nowhere he grabs a chain saw. He
yanks several times at the starter cord until the saw roars to life. Its metal
teeth bite and hack at my dress, tearing it to shreds. Exhaust smoke and
floating shreds of cloth fill the room. *Isn't it romantic...*

I peel off my panties before he gets any ideas about taking the chain saw
to them. And in no time, we're going at it like a couple of porn stars being
paid by the orgasm.

Hours later, utterly spent, we lie panting next to each other. I turn over
onto my stomach and languidly brush his chest with my fingertips. "How
come you never take off your t-shirt?" I ask.

Crispin shakes his head. "I can't tell you. It's part of my mysterious,
melancholy past that makes me so fascinating."

"Oh." *Maybe he's got a hairy back, like an ape.*

"So, was it good for you?" He's actually smiling.

"Which one?" I answer playfully. "The first climax? The second? The
twenty-ninth?"

"Ah, Anesthesia, you are so naughty. I shall have to punish you."
Crispin whacks a frying pan across my butt, which shakes like a bowl full of
jelly. "Did that hurt?" he asks eagerly.

"Nope."

He hits me harder. I smile. Another whack, even harder. He's getting
irked, I can tell – so just to please him, I squeak "Ouch."

He smirks. "Did *that* hurt?"

"Yes, master," I whisper.

"Good." He settles back on the pillow. "Since you're new to this, I'll go
easy on you today. But next time around, we'll get serious."

Gulp. "How serious?"

His eyes narrow, and his grin seems positively cruel. "Maybe something
like slowwwwly ripping a Band-Aid off your arm."

***

By the end of the next day, Crispin has sent me a new iPhone, a genuine
cashmere sweater with matching mittens, and a travel martini kit. My
subconscious comes out of hiding and whispers, "You shouldn't accept
expensive gifts from him, you ho!" She's probably right, but I really need
the mittens.

My last day of work at Dretzka's leaves me emotionally drained. I can
hardly believe this is the last time I'll be dusting plaster mannequins and

rearranging galoshes so old their rubber is literally crumbling. When my shift ends, the owners call me into the office and surprise me with a check for $2.56.

That evening, Lurch comes to collect my Corvair. I wave goodbye as he drives away. Too late, I remember the rust holes in Gertrude's floorboards and exhaust pipe; I should've warned Lurch to keep the windows rolled down.

A barrage of emails from Crispin over the next few days alternately pleases and annoys me. He wants to know what I'm doing, who I'm with, and whether I'm still binging on M&Ms. I put my English degree to good use, dazzling him with witty replies like "Oh yeah? Says who?" and "So's your old man."

***

It's Saturday evening. Catherine Cadaver, Crispin's brother Elliott Ness and I have settled into our new place. Delafield looks like an old New England town that inexplicably sprang up in the Midwest. It's all antique shops, brick crosswalks, art galleries, cute boutiques and organic grocery stores. I feel like I need a passport to come here.

Our new three-bedroom apartment is all imported wallpaper and polished wood. Too bad the wallpaper is on the floor and the polished wood is on the walls; the subcontractors screwed up.

Elliott departs early that night. "Sorry, hon," he tells Catherine Cadaver, "but there's no way I can get out of this family get-together. Our sister Peeia just flew in from Paris. You know how it is."

Catherine Cadaver nods, as if anyone we ever knew had any relatives outside Cudahy. "I'm counting the hours until you return," she coos. "I'll keep the vibrator on standby." Ugh. Their sweet talk is so icky.

"Laters, babe." Elliott blows her a kiss, and Catherine Cadaver pretends to feel the kiss landing on her cheek. Barf! Okay, so I'm a little jealous. Unlike his brother, Elliott isn't afraid to show his feelings in public. He doesn't even make Catherine Cadaver walk five paces behind him.

***

As the week goes on, I see several sides of Crispin BenGay:

Domineering... A long, hard session with the toilet plunger teaches me unquestioning obedience.

Romantic... Crispin reveals that he can do a mean polka. We dance naked in his kitchen to the sweet strains of Frankie Yankovic.

Alcoholic... Every occasion – whether it's getting out of bed, finishing a crossword puzzle, or checking the weather forecast – calls for wine. I'm

45

learning to distinguish between the expensive vintages Crispin serves and my old favorites, Mogan David and Ripple.

One night Crispin takes me to visit his family in Whitefish Bay. His parents' home, a Lake Michigan bluffside mansion, screams "old money," "new money," and "ancient plumbing."

Crispin's mother, Dr. Grace Whatever-the-frack-hyphen-hyphen, greets us at the door. "Come in, darlings," she says, giving each of us a big hug. "I was just finishing the guest list for the Symphony Ball. Do you think we should invite Mayor Maier?"

"Mother, he's been dead for nearly 20 years," Crispin says, rolling his eyes.

"Oh," she says distractedly, "then he probably wouldn't come."

Behind Dr. Grace stands a man in a tuxedo. "Ana," Crispin says, "this is my father, Dirk Diggler BenGay. Dad, this is Anesthesia Peel."

Dirk shakes my hand. "Pleased to meet you, Ana." He straightens the dark lapels of his tux. "Sorry I haven't had a chance to dress for dinner. I just got home from the Grain Exchange."

Seeing my puzzled look, Crispin pulls me aside. "I know what you're thinking: *Didn't that opulent trading pit go out of business in 1935?* But Dad likes to hang out among the frescoes and colossal faux-marble pillars, pretending he's Andrew Carnegie, so we humor him."

"Actually, I was thinking I need to use the bathroom," I tell Crispin. "That bottle of wine we finished off in the limo just hit my bladder."

But as Crispin begins giving me directions to the can, someone screeches, "Is that *her?!*" Everyone turns as a tall, striking brunette barrels down the hallway. She grabs me in a bear hug. "Anesthesia! Crispin has told us so much about you. He says you work at Dretzka's. What a kidder!"

"Ana," Crispin mutters, "this is my sister, Peeia."

Peeia grabs my hand and drags me into the living room. It's all tasteful creams, browns, and pale blues. No furniture, just colors. Catherine Cadaver and Crispin's brother Elliott Ness are already in there, admiring a porcelain tea set. Probably priceless artwork, but it looks like something my Aunt Berniece would find at Goodwill.

Dinner is interminable. I can barely choke down this oh-so-fashionable food: salad made with arguable lettuce or whatever they call it, and no croutons, and a bitter vinegary dressing … skimpy baby potatoes without gravy… measly quail drumsticks… and goat cheese – for dessert! As we eat, silly Peeia prattles on about her recent trip to Paris, giggling constantly and lapsing into French. Gag.

After dinner, Crispin announces we're taking a stroll in the garden. Yeah, right. That bulge in his trousers makes it clear I won't be picking petunias.

Sure enough, the moment the potting shed door slams behind us,

Crispin jumps my bones. Luckily I don't shatter into a million pieces this time, because Peeia comes looking for us a little while later, and those shattered pieces would have given us away.

Mercifully, the evening ends early. Dr. Grace Overachiever-Hoggenzschwartz is called to the hospital for an emergency hangnail case. Dirk says he's meeting Cornelius Vanderbilt at the club to sip glasses of port and discuss a new railway line they're planning in North Carolina.

Crispin and I slip into the limo, and Lurch drives us back to Delafield.

***

Crispin surprises me that night when we return to his condo. "What do you say we bypass the Playroom of Pain and go straight to bed?"

"Are you mellowing out?" I tease.

"Anesthesia, I…" Looking confused, he runs a hand through his hair. Two hands. Then three. Gee, he really *is* confused.

Leading him to the bedroom, I whisper, "I just want to make love without pain, then fall asleep together and wake up with you next to me."

His face registers disgust. "Ugh. You're really kinky." He opens a dresser drawer and pulls out a t-shirt, tossing it at me. I guess this is supposed to be my nightshirt.

Flouncing into the bathroom, I remove my dress, pantyhose and girdle, then try to squeeze into Crispin's t-shirt. Way too small. It makes me look like an arm-wrestler's bicep with a teeny wristband on top. Sighing, I pull it off again and return to the bedroom in all my glorious nakedness.

"Look, Crispin," I say, "if we're gonna go steady, I need to know more about you. Why are you so melancholy all the time? What's your big bad secret? I can't live with all this mystery."

Crispin, lying on the bed, looks up from his *Wall Street Journal,* eyes wary. "You wouldn't really leave me, would you? After all I've bought for you?"

Hmmm, he's got a point there. The laptop, the BMW…but then I remember tonight's BenGay family dinner – stingy, almost food-free – and realize it epitomizes all that Crispin can't or won't give me. Would I leave him?

In the menacing tone I've used on would-be shoplifters at Dretzka's, I reply, "I might."

Crispin runs multiple hands through his hair, still going through that inner struggle. Finally he sighs.

"All right," he says. "I'll level with you. Before Grace and Dirk adopted me, I had a miserable childhood."

"Miserable…how?" I press. "Were you starved? Beaten?"

"No. Worse than that." Crispin hangs his head. "I grew up on the wrong side of the tracks."

I gasp. "You mean…?"

"Yes," he whispers. "South Milwaukee."

Ohmigosh. This is like Oliver Twist, Little Orphan Annie and Bruce Wayne rolled into one. Especially Bruce Wayne, considering how he grew up to be Batman, handsome and filthy rich.

"Crispin, I'm so sorry," I say. "I had no idea."

"Well, now you do." He slips out of bed and wanders into the hallway. Before too long, the haunting strains of "Who Stole the Kishka?" tell me that Crispin and his accordion are in a dark, scary place where I can't reach him.

CHAPTER 8
UNHAPPY ENDING

The next morning I awaken alone, in Crispin's bed. Using the GPS on my new iPhone, I track him through the cavernous condo. He's in the study, which is all hardwood and antique office furniture and walls papered with $100 bills.

Crispin sits at a desk, talking on the phone. I eavesdrop. "What's your market cap, prime minister?" Crispin says. "I want to buy you out....Of course your country's for sale. Everything's for sale when the price is right....I don't take no for an answer....What would it take for us to close the deal today?"

Crispin's face reddens. He holds out the receiver, staring at it. "That S.O.B. just hung up on me!" he shouts.

"Erm..." I say, momentarily forgetting that I'm not an English twit. I feel a sudden urge to consume Twinings English Tea (bag out) and throw toys from my pram.

"I hate it when people won't let me buy them out!" Crispin lets loose a string of profanities.

"Anything I can do?" I say meekly.

"Yeah," he snarls. "Get up on that desk and let me boink you. At least I can control something around here."

"OK." I hop onto the desk, and it crashes beneath my weight. I bite my lower lip. "Erm...I hope that wasn't a priceless antique."

Crispin glowers at me. Maybe it's the phone hangup, or the ruined desk, or (oops!) my irritating habit of biting my lip – but he is seriously ticked off, and moments later he really lets me have it. Let's just say I never imagined a Rolodex would even *fit* down there.

***

Over the next few days, I interview for internships at McDonald's, Burger King and Wendy's. The McDonald's opening seems especially promising, and I allow myself to fantasize a little bit; after all, I look pretty good in orange.

Things improve in the Crispin department as well. He loosens up and confides some truly romantic things to me:

"If you don't want to be bound and gagged in a crate, then I won't bind and gag you and throw you in a crate."

"Don't think of yourself as my whore. Think of yourself as someone who has sex with me, and then I pay her."

"Where were you from 11:07 to 11:08 a.m. yesterday? Your GPS was turned off."

"Mrs. Robinson is still my friend and business partner. We deal in child slavery in southeast Asia. We haven't had sex with each other in years, though – ever since her husband found out about me."

"Having your period? Here, let me throw that used tampon in the toilet. I'm so filthy rich I don't worry about clogging the plumbing. My people will take care of it."

"Yes, I enjoy beating you, and I want to hurt you. But don't worry, I have no intention of killing you. Except maybe when you bite your lip."

Oy vey, what a man. He brings out so many new sides of myself I never knew before: sex slave, domestic abuse victim, hooker-in-training, paranoid girlfriend, slut.

But as the days pass, Crispin turns moody again, becoming even more of an a-hole than usual. To cheer him, I show up at his condo with a novel suggestion: "Let's have sex!"

So we do it – first in the foyer, then in his bedroom, then the shower, the wine cellar, the broom closet, and finally inside his kitchen's enormous walk-in freezer. I have so many orgasms, moregasms and s'moregasms that by number 18 or so, they become routine boregasms.

Crispin studies me closely, his eyes hooded like a Ku Klux Klansman. "Bored?" he asks.

"Well, sorta," I admit.

"Come," he says, dragging me down the hall, "let's visit the Red Room of Pain."

"Uh, can we have something to eat first?" I ask, but he's not listening. Before I know it he's hauled me into the Red Room, and I'm buck naked, bent forward over a red velvet chaise lounge. Crispin has trussed my wrists and ankles together, making me feel like a Thanksgiving turkey.

He stands behind me, and I can almost feel him staring at my bare backside. I've been told it resembles the Allen-Bradley clock tower: a huge, round white orb, glowing in the night. If this doesn't turn him off, nothing will. Maybe he'll get nauseated and decide to let me go.

"This is it, Anesthesia," he growls. "The moment of truth."

"What..." My mouth is dry. I swallow and begin again: "What are you going to do?"

"I'm going to beat you within an inch of your life." For some reason, this doesn't sound very sensuous.

"With your hand?" I ask hopefully.

"No."

"With the frying pan?"

"No. With a belt."

Suddenly the belt *thwacks* against my backside. Pain!

"Stop it!" I cry.

"Relax, Ana. Stay 'in the moment,' " Crispin mutters through clenched teeth.

Thwack. Thwack. The leather bites into my flesh. "Aaaaaaiiieee!" I scream.

"Ana!" Crispin's voice is heavy with lust. "Be. Here. Now."

"I *am* here now, you pervert!" I yell. "But I'd rather be in Cudahy!"

Thwack. Thwack. Thwack. Thwack. These heavy blows must be drawing blood. Where will I find a Band-Aid large enough for my Allen-Bradley behind?

Finally, the whipping ceases. Crispin loosens the restraints on my wrists and ankles. "You. Are. So. Sexy," he mutters, panting heavily.

"You. Are. So. *Sick*," I retort. "I've had it, Crispin. This relationship is kaput." I gather up my clothing, lumber down the hallway and lock myself in the circus-theme bedroom. Finally, alone here, I allow myself to burst into sobs.

What the hell was I thinking? Sure, he's hot in bed, but he's also a sadistic control freak. A creepy stalker. Emotionally, he's Scrooge. Worst of all, he gets his kicks from hurting me – really hurting me.

And to think I wasted an entire three weeks of my life on this jerk.

I stare at the mirror, still aware that this is a cliché – but a necessary cliché, bringing me full circle. A red-nosed, blubbering wreck stares back at me.

Slowly, I get dressed. My inner goddess is already calculating how many gallons of Häagen-Dazs the recovery process will take.

My heart heavy, I shuffle through Crispin's condo for the last time. I draw my hand across my nose, wiping away the snot.

Crispin stands in the foyer, absentmindedly whapping the folded belt against his palm. We face each other.

"Must you go?" His face is anguished. "There's still a lot of life left in this belt."

He's got a lot of nerve, looking anguished. I'm the one whose backside feels like it's just gone through a table saw at the meatpacking plant.

"Goodbye, Crispin," I whisper.

Lurch brings the limo around. I huddle in the back as he drives down the street to my new place.

As we pass the brand new fake old-fashioned street lamps, I wish I'd never moved with Catherine Cadaver to fashionable Delafield, which doesn't have any bowling alleys or laundromats. No meatpacking plant to give the place character. No frigid wind whistling off Lake Michigan. No taverns on every single corner, where everybody knows your name as well as how many beers you can drink before passing out.

Seized by a sudden inspiration, I tap on the glass separating the passenger compartment from the front seat.

Lurch picks up a phone receiver, and his voice buzzes in the ceiling speaker: "Yes, ma'am?"

"Lurch, take me to Cudahy." My voice is firm with conviction. "I'm going home."

THE END

FINAL WORDS FROM THE AUTHOR

Thank you for your patience. I hope you found this parody somewhat less tedious than the original.

If by some fluke you actually liked this story, you may also like my Spoofbook series:
--*Arts and Crap: A Spoofbook on Arts and Crafts*
--*For Pets' Sake: A Spoofbook on Pets*
--*White Lace and Panic: A Spoofbook on Weddings*
--*Gimme Shelter: A Spoofbook on Home Decorating*
All are available in Kindle format at Amazon.com for just 99 cents each.

Also, please check out my silly merchandise at www.carsonmania.com. You'll wonder how you lived this long without a dog-themed "To lick or not to lick" dishwasher magnet. The website also features my ridiculous CarsonmaniaBlog and Twitter feed.

Laters, babe.

Leah Carson

www.ingramcontent.com/pod-product-compliance
Lightning Source LLC
Chambersburg PA
CBHW060623030426
42337CB00018B/3165